This special book belongs to

Child's Name _____

Date of Birth _____

Your
Baby's
Photo

"The Class of _____"
(add 18 to the year of your baby's birth)

"The Class With CONNECTIONS"

This book has been funded in part by

Nemours | Nemours Children's Clinic

Nemours Children's Clinic is a division of Nemours, one of the nation's largest children's health systems headquartered in Jacksonville, Florida. Nemours owns and operates the Alfred I. duPont Children's Hospital in Wilmington Delaware and major specialty centers in Florida (Jacksonville, Orlando, and Pensacola), Pennsylvania (Philadelphia and Bryn Mawr), and New Jersey (Atlantic City and Voorhees).

For more information about the Nemours please visit www.nemours.org.

Thanks to Arnold Palmer Hospital for Children & Women,

5932-69455 8/05

Dhaysia has a
chance to grow up.

Little Dhaysia was born with a life-threatening lung infection.

Fortunately, she was at Arnold Palmer Hospital where doctors are prepared for such emergencies. Once in the Level III Neonatal Intensive Care Unit, Dhaysia was supported by an advanced system that breathed for her until her lungs could heal.

This year, the Neonatal Intensive Care Unit celebrates 30 years of giving hope to parents – and children another chance at life.

arnoldpalmerhospital.org

Arnold Palmer Hospital
FOR CHILDREN • WOMEN
Part of Orlando Regional Healthcare

Building Baby's BRAIN POWER

Hundreds of One-Minute Brain Stimulating Activities for Baby's First Years

by

Noreen Darragh Lantry, RN

and

Kathy Icardi Hummel, MSW, L.C.S.W.

For information write to: BETA Center, Inc.
4680 Lake Underhill Road
Orlando, Florida 32807
407-277-1942

DISCLAIMER: The author and publisher disclaim responsibility for any adverse effects resulting directly or indirectly from the activities described and illustrated herein, or from the reader's misunderstanding of the text.

GENDER: The author wishes to respect and recognize the value of each gender equally, male and female. You will notice the activities refer to her or him. Both genders are used alternatively.

PROCEEDS from the sale of this book directly benefit at-risk families who receive services from BETA Center, Inc., a non-profit organization. For more information, visit our web site at www.betacenter.org.

**THIS BOOK IS AVAILABLE AT QUANTITY
DISCOUNTS FOR EDUCATIONAL USE.**

ISBN 0-9671289-1-9

Dedication

This book is for all children
and the people who care for them . . .

And in particular for the children
we cannot afford to leave behind.

Acknowledgements

This book was a vision that became a reality through the hard work and dedication of many BETA Center staff members, volunteers and special friends. First and foremost among them are the book's co-authors, Katherine ("Kathy") Icardi Hummel, our executive vice president for clinical services, and Noreen Lantry, child development specialist, who spearheads our parent/child interaction programs. At BETA Center, caring and hard work are the hallmarks of serving those in need, and these two women exemplify this philosophy. We are so grateful to them for sharing their talents with us.

The leadership and inspiration of Ray Larsen, BETA Center's former executive director, was instrumental in the initial conception and development of the book. When I took over as chief executive officer, I quickly became convinced of the value of this project, and made it a mission to bring it to fruition. Tom Connellan, a local author and motivational speaker, has been a valuable volunteer "mentor" for us on how to package, market and distribute the book.

There are many others, too — unfortunately too numerous to mention here — whose support and commitment made this dream happen. They also deserve our most heartfelt thanks.

We did it!

Hope Kramer, President & CEO
BETA Center, Inc.
April 5, 2004

Table of Contents

Attention Parents
of Newborns!

Brand new babies will sleep most of the time.
They usually wake for a short time to eat, burp
and be changed.

A newborn needs GENTLE stimulation,
like holding, rocking, lullaby singing, soft words,
soft light and gentle touch.

When baby begins to focus and be awake more,
you may choose to add more involved activities
and begin using this book!

Introduction to...

Brain Power

What Is BRAIN POWER?

Brain Power is building brain connections that will make your baby smarter, happier and healthier. You help brain connections happen with YOUR

EYE CONTACT

TOUCH

PLAY

SMILE

Brain **CONNECTION** Facts

The kind of information that goes into
the brain affects its actual structure.

"CONNECTIONS" between brain cells
(called synapses) are activated and increased
when you PLAY and INTERACT.

The only way to keep connections growing
is repeated play, communication and attention
to your infant.

Brain **CONNECTION** Facts

The number of connections between
brain cells depends upon the number
of experiences each child has.

The number of connections between the cells
can keep multiplying for up to 4 years.

From birth to age 12 the brain is like a "sponge,"
quickly absorbing information.

Emotional Brain Facts

Scientists can see emotions being formed in the brain.

Children can learn to speak and understand emotions and ideas . . . even if they never learn to read and write.

When you talk to your baby, you begin to share your beliefs and values with your baby.

25% of parents do not know their actions can affect the intelligence of their children.

Keep practicing . . . Keep playing . . . You and your baby will be better for it!

About You ...
BRAIN POWER and Baby

If it doesn't feel easy to talk and play with your baby ...
you are not alone. Many parents (60%) think it's hard
and sometimes silly to talk and play with their baby.

So if you sometimes feel that way, know that it is a
normal feeling. But, you should know that not talking
and playing with your baby limits their opportunities.
If you do talk and play with baby, you are building
baby's brain power.

Many people who felt silly at first found these activities
so easy to do ... it became part of their daily routine.

Learning for the very young occurs best through play!

BRAIN BUILDING Facts

Humans have 100 billion brain cells.

Newborns start with 50 trillion connections between these cells.

Good brain development is about making sure that many of these connections are made possible!

Care, love and stimulation need to start EARLY. This helps ensure the life and growth of the brain connections.

7

CONNECTING With Baby

Your undivided ATTENTION to your baby is the
most powerful connection.

Baby can tell when you are being respectful,
honest and sincere.

Your baby will only CONNECT when he or she feels
secure and safe. That connection is the connection
that builds BRAIN POWER.

Your baby makes connections when a caring
adult follows the simple formula on the next page.

The **BRAIN BUILDING** Formula

DESCRIBE — Size; Color; Shape.

ASK QUESTIONS — "Do you like this ball?"
"Do you want to play?"

REINFORCE — "This ball is round,
a football, fun."

LET BABY EXPLORE — Find a safe place for baby to discover under your watchful eye.

PACE — Are you allowing your baby to play as long as she is interested?

PROVIDE CHOICES — Let your baby pick the ball or rattle he wants to play with.

REPEAT — "This is a block." Say "block." Repeating is a way we learn to make connections.

The **ONE-MINUTE ACTIVITY**

A one-minute activity is a quick, simple and easy way for you to stimulate your baby's brain.

All parents and caregivers can follow the one-minute daily activities.

A one-minute activity every day is not intended to be ALL your child requires from you.

It is an extra special addition to the time and caring you give to your baby all day, every day.

During The
ONE-MINUTE ACTIVITY

SMILE . . . PRAISE . . . HELP

This is your baby's time to show you
how she experiences the world.

NEVER . . . scold . . . yell . . . or say "no."
YOU are your child's first teacher.

Your guidance will help your baby feel like
he can do more. A child's feeling of
SELF-ESTEEM begins at infancy . . .

YOU are the person to help
your baby feel important.
YOUR FACE MAKES HER SMILE!

How To Get
The Best Results

Read your baby's signals . . .
It is important that you watch your baby's
behavior. Even small babies will tell you when
they are ready. Baby will signal when it's time to stop
(rubbing eyes . . . fussing . . . turning away).

Set up a good environment...
Baby should be rested, not crying or hungry.
Baby should be alert and happy
(smiling . . . reaching out).

A good environment for learning is:

QUIET
CALM
FREE OF CLUTTER

How To Get The Best Results

Make sure your baby is in a comfortable position
to see ... hear ... and feel your responses.

Let Your Baby Take The Lead!

Let your baby touch and become familiar with
the objects before interaction.

IF your baby does not respond ...
STOP ... come back again to the interaction.

Your baby is always checking things out around him ...
Does this feel good? Should I reach out? Is it safe?
Is mommy or daddy caring about me?

Some Important Tips

Babies learn by imitating, repeating, interacting, experimenting and putting things in their mouth.

Putting things to their mouth is an important part of infant learning, but . . . KEEP IT SAFE!

Repeat . . . Repeat . . . Repeat.
Repeat your baby's activities, words and sounds.
Hold an object about 7 to 9 inches from your baby's face so baby can focus.

Every activity in this book will involve one or more of the FIVE SENSES: sight, smell, hearing, taste and touch.

The FIVE SENSES

It is through the FIVE SENSES that the brain receives information.

A child is able to discover through the FIVE SENSES the characteristics of objects such as color, size, texture, smell, sound and movement.

You want to teach your baby using one, two or all of the senses.

HEARING   VISION   SMELL   TASTE   TOUCH

Each activity tells you which sense is helping baby learn.

FIVE SENSES Exercise

Here's an example of how to use the FIVE SENSES (using the activity on page 132).

- Sit across from your baby and <u>look</u> into his eyes.
- Show baby the banana, holding it 7 to 9 inches away. Let baby's eyes <u>focus</u>.
- Help baby <u>touch</u> the banana. Say descriptive words like, "cool, smooth, rough on the end."
- <u>Say</u> the word "banana." <u>Explain</u> that it is a fruit, it is yellow with brown spots, it is about 5 inches long and round. Let baby put his lips to the banana skin.
- Does the banana make a <u>sound</u>? If you peel it, is there a soft <u>sound</u>?
- Show baby and describe how you peel the banana. What do you <u>see</u> inside?
- Let the baby <u>smell</u> the peeled fruit. Let him <u>touch</u> the soft texture.

For more information about the FIVE SENSES, see page 211.

16

Setting Up The
ONE-MINUTE ACTIVITY

➡ Read the introductory material.
➡ Read the activity for the day.
➡ Decide where you are going to play.
➡ Gather the necessary supplies.
➡ Place this book near you and your baby.
➡ Help your baby feel comfortable.
➡ Place your baby safely across from you.
➡ Make eye contact with your baby.

Don't Forget To Read
The BRAIN FACTS On
The Activity Pages.

BRAIN POWER
Activities

Do an activity every day.
Don't forget . . . there is more information and
references in the last section of the book.

Print the year on a piece of paper, for example: 2005.

Tell baby what year it is.

Have baby watch as you trace and say each number.

Look at baby and smile.

Tell baby 5 things that will happen this year!

Show baby how DIFFERENT actions feel.
Use your hands in his.

Try: touch, hold, pat, swing hands, hold hands.

Name the action.

As you repeat, let baby experience the feeling.

Repeat 3 times.

- Sit across from baby and look at her.

Talk . . . tell her something funny that happened to you.

Let her see you laugh!

21

Make eye contact.

Tell baby how beautiful or handsome she/he is.

Tell baby 5 things you like about her/him.

Repeat 2 times.

22

Brain Fact:
Infants "store" ALL words
in their memory for later use.

Hold baby up to a fogged bathroom mirror.

Tell baby how it got that way.

Squeak the mirror and wipe it clear.

Explain to baby about the beautiful people
who have appeared!

23

Gently shake a rattle 8 inches from baby's face.

Shake it to the left . . . shake it to the right.

Shake the rattle behind the baby.

Help baby find it, touch it, reach for it and hold it.

Repeat 2 times.

Brain Fact:
Pleasing music is created by string sounds that bear simple mathematical relationships to one another.

Turn on, or hum, some nice relaxing music.

Hold baby and look into his eyes, smiling.

Spend a "soothing minute" together.

Sit in front of baby.

Get eye contact and attention.

Show her a small ball ... place the ball in baby's palm.

Gently mold her fingers around the ball.

Say "ball."

Say "it's round."

Repeat several times.

Sit or lie opposite baby.

Make eye contact and "talk."

Make a "raspberry" noise. Repeat.

Make a "whistle." Repeat.

Push breath out. Repeat.

Say "blah, blah, blah."

Between each sound, watch baby for a response.

Mark a balloon with a marker in a contrasting color.

Tie the balloon to a chair.

Place baby where he can observe.

Gently blow on the balloon . . . gently bob the balloon.

Repeat several times.

Sit baby across from you.

Show her a loaf of bread — the many pieces and the crinkly wrapper.

Take out one slice, name it.

Smell it and pass it under the baby's nose.

Fold it in half, let baby smell.

Tear it in four pieces, let baby see and smell.

You eat a piece of the slice. Let baby see you enjoy ... mmm!

Let baby experience different wet textures
on his arm or hand.

Tell baby what you're doing . . . go slowly.

Touch with a warm washcloth. Stroke with lotion.
Dab with oil. Dribble water from a warm cloth.
Describe sensations.

Repeat 3 times.

Brain Fact: The caress of another releases hormones to clear the mind.

Sit across from baby.

Start with yourself, and then with baby.

Touch your hair, then baby's ... your mouth, then baby's and so on.

Go from head to toe.

Tell baby what you are doing.

Show baby a picture of Martin Luther King, Jr.

Share pictures and descriptions of people of different countries and ethnicities.

Show baby the ways people are the same.

Martin Luther King, Jr. said, "I have a dream."

Tell baby about your "dreams" for his future.

Brain Fact:
If baby gestures towards a bottle, and Mom responds, it increases a child's desire to communicate.

Let baby sit where he can see you do the dishes.

Name and show each item ... plates, cups, glasses, pots, sponge and soap.

Talk about dirty and clean.

Thank baby for keeping you company!

Show baby grooming items.

Name the comb, the brush, shampoo bottle, toothbrush, mirror.

Show how they work, how they smell.

Let baby hear the teeth and bristles of the comb and toothbrush as you run your finger over them.

Repeat 2 times.

34

Brain Fact: Repetition helps language skills.

Take 3 blank pieces of paper.

Draw and color 3 circles on each one (all red, all black, all green).

Show each paper separately.

Point to the colors and say them.

Trace the shape and say it.

Watch which one baby likes best.

Repeat 2 times.

35

Let baby enjoy the feeling and fragrance of a pretty scarf.

Is it new or does it smell like Mom's perfume?

Guess what smell baby will like best!

Baby will enjoy the soft caress of a scarf as you let it drift and travel along baby's arms, legs and head.

Repeat as baby enjoys.

Sit on the floor with baby.

Make eye contact and alert him to a toy nearby.

Say "toy" and point to it.

Then let him see you cover the toy with a cloth.

Ask, "Where is the toy?"

With baby watching, remove the cloth.

Say, "There's the toy!"

Repeat 4 times.

Brain Fact: Studies show that infants prefer the sweet taste of milk.

At meal time have baby sit with you.

It's important to keep this family time pleasant.

Describe the color and taste of milk.

Does baby like her milk?

Tell your baby how you know she does.

Place these things next to baby:

a fresh cotton pillow case, a clean sock,
a sweater, a blanket, and a silk scarf.

Help baby feel and smell each material.

Repeat 2 times.

Show baby an apple.

Describe the apple's color.

Peel the apple.

Show how we eat it.

Let baby watch, smell and touch.

Give baby a taste (baby food or fruit depends on baby's age).

Show baby 2 toys, holding one in each hand.

Bring one forward for baby to see and describe it.

Bring the other forward and describe it.

Let baby look ... observe which one baby looks at the most.

Tell baby what you observed.

Repeat 3 times.

Brain Fact:
If baby feels and hears,
he/she remembers longer.

Sit with your baby.

Touch, stroke and count . . . ears, cheeks,
shoulders, arms, each hand and each finger.

Name these.

Repeat 3 times.

Say your baby's name frequently.

When baby responds to his or her name,
respond appropriately . . .

Smile, hug, praise!

Read a page from a favorite book.

Re-read the page 4 times.

Sit across from baby.

Make 5 different sounds from 5 different places
(tap on the table, scratch the rug, knock on the wall,
drum fingers, say hello).

Observe baby.

Describe how you make the noise.

Repeat.

Sit across from baby.

Make eye contact.

SMILE!

Let baby see you wink.

Alternate eyes, saying ... "this is a wink ... THIS is a wink."

Repeat 8 times.

Draw many red hearts on a paper.

Show baby . . . make eye contact and say "I love you."

"You make me happy when _____."

"You have pretty _____."

"You are special to me and _____."

Repeat 3 times.

Show baby 5 pictures of animals.

For example: Show baby a picture of a dog.

Say "dog." Then say its sound — "woof woof."

Repeat the 5 pictures and sounds 3 times.

Put on some music . . . you can try rock or hip-hop.

Dance with baby, but keep the movement gentle.

Baby enjoys being close to you!

Sit across from baby.

Try on several hats.

Try a baseball cap, visor, paper hat or scarf.

Talk to baby about the hats and her reaction!

Place baby in a seat across from you.

When he is watching you, blow on several different items.

For example: a ribbon, an envelope, a tissue,
a pen, a magazine page.

Talk about what happens.

Try each item 2 times.

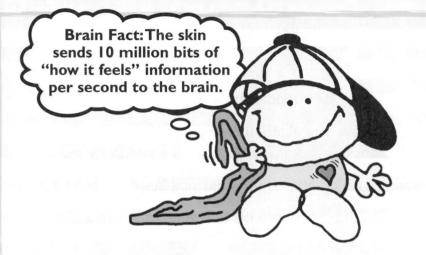

Let baby experience pleasant skin sensations.

Gently stroke baby's hand or arm.

Pass a cloth over his hands or arms.

Caress with a soft cloth.

Say "soft" in a gentle voice.

Repeat on each arm.

Show baby a picture of the first United States president, George Washington. (Look on a dollar bill.)

Say, "president, dollar, green."

Show one dollar. Say "one."

Show three dollars. Say "three."

If you have time today, do 2 activities!

While baby is alert and sitting facing you,
show her the different shoe types from your closet.

Say, "These are high heeled shoes.
Mommy wears them dancing."

Or, "This white shoe is a tennis shoe and
I wear it when I go on long walks."

You might add: "work shoe," "pump,"
"saddle shoe," "boot" and others.

Get a book or cut out magazine pictures of a dog, a cat, a bird or farm animals.

Read with baby looking at pictures as you point to them, naming the animals.

Sit across from baby and make eye contact.

Pull out your wallet or purse.

Show baby every item that comes out!

Name each item, and put it back in.

Repeat.

Holding baby, walk through the house.

Find every mirror ... stop in front of each.

Help baby see himself and you.

Say "mirror ... look it's you and me."

Repeat 2 times.

Slice an onion.

Pass it near baby's nose and note baby's reaction.

Describe the odor and what the onion is used for.

Repeat 3 times.

Get a paper plate and a dark marker.

Draw a pleasant face on the plate.

Hold the plate up for baby to see.

Does he look interested? Probably.

Allow baby time to look at the features.

Repeat 4 times.

Show one macaroni; then fill a bowl.

Run your fingers through it to make noise.

Let baby try . . . help baby feel, and cover baby's fingers
with the macaronies.

Help baby make a noise against the sides of the bowl.

Repeat 3 times.

Sit baby near you to see 5 containers.

Name and describe each container.

Plastic, thin glass, metal, cardboard, thick glass.

Tap each with a spoon, making your own sounds.

Repeat 3 times.

Show baby 5 favorite toys.

Name and show each one with its noise.

Repeat 3 times.

(Try 2 different rattles, beans or rice in a jar, a bell, a music box or a push-pull toy.)

Sit with baby on your lap.

Look at a magazine together.

Point and describe the colors, places and objects you see.

Baby will enjoy hearing your voice.

With baby sitting across from you and watching,
name a round object. Tell him what you're going to do.
Drop the round object from eye level to the floor.

Try a tennis ball, cotton ball, tinfoil ball or balloon.

Repeat slowly 3 times.

Sit baby on your lap.

If baby allows, touch each toe.

Say "toe."

Count them.

Tell and show baby how many toes each foot has.

Repeat 2 times.

Tell baby you are making bubbles.

Show her how you lather your hands with dishwashing soap. Show baby how the bubbles can travel by waving your hand. Repeat.

Let baby touch a bubble. Repeat.

Blow the bubbles from your hand.

While baby is watching, repeat the word "bubble."

Gather a few items from the refrigerator.

Try mustard, ketchup, mayo, barbecue sauce.

Sit baby across from you.

Pass a spoonful of one food at a time under
baby's nose. Name the smell.

Allow time for baby's reaction.

Repeat 2 times.

Sit baby across from you. Show baby gestures that people use. Repeat and explain each gesture.

Lean forward and say "I move closer when I want to share." Reach out and say "I reach out to show I want something." Shrug shoulders and say "I do this when I don't know."

Shake head and say "this means no."

Smile! Repeat 4 times.

Choose 3 toys.

Lie on the floor next to baby.

Now you can see what he sees!

Move the toys across your sight.

Are they too close? . . . too far? . . . too loud?

Enjoy each toy together.

Look and smile.

Sing 3 favorite songs daily.

Encourage baby to imitate words and sounds.

Watch while baby listens!

Cut a lemon.

Pass the wet side under baby's nose.

Name the odor and describe it.

What is baby's reaction?

Repeat 4 times, naming the smell.

Place baby on your lap. Look at a magazine together.

Let baby watch while you trace circular items with your finger, saying "round" or "circle."

Find 15 items that are round, such as wheels, watches, hamburgers and faces.

If baby can, have him trace each circle with his fingers.

Take a walk around your own "art museum."

Point out all the pictures and say "pictures."

The pictures might be of flowers, animals, people, etc.

Describe each one, like . . .

"Me and Grandma. Our dresses are red.
I graduated that day."

Baby will look if you point and talk.

Sit across from baby and make eye contact.

Use your hands to cover your face.

Uncover and say "peek-a-boo." Repeat 3 times.

Then place your hands in front of and block baby's face.

Fan your hands to the sides revealing baby's face and eyes.

Smile . . . say "peek-a-boo." Repeat 3 times.

Gather 6 pieces of clothing —

2 from mom, 2 from baby, 2 from dad or sister.

Name the owner as baby smells each piece of clothing.

Repeat 2 times.

Take a white sock.

Try it on your hand to see where the face goes.

Draw a face on the sock.

Have your "puppet" talk nice to baby!

Sit with baby, looking into his eyes.

Tell him about something that was hard for you today.

Talk about how it made you feel.

Hold baby's hand and kiss it!

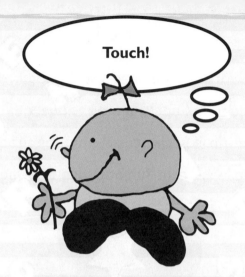

Walk with baby outside.

Point out the pretty spring leaves and flowers.

Bring them close.

Describe their names and colors.

Touch baby's hand with soft greens or flowers.

What does baby do?

Most babies like all music. Try jazz, classical and rock.

Sit with baby and enjoy the music.

Hold baby's hand and gently swing hands or arms
to the tempo.

Today during the change or bath, name every body part, head to toe.

Tell baby how every part is good and how you love them.

Show baby an ORANGE.

Say the name "orange."

Roll it and let baby smell it.

Just a little taste with the tongue!

Repeat 4 times.

Pop some popcorn.

Help baby see and let him listen.

Describe what is happening.

How does he react?

Sit across from baby.

Look at each other.

Practice simple sounds:

La la la . . . ba ba ba . . . ta ta ta . . . rah rah rah . . .
ma ma ma . . . da da da . . .

After each sound, wait for baby to talk!

Repeat 3 times.

When baby is sitting across from you and looking,
show her 3 kinds of books.

Try a hardcover, a magazine and a paperback.

Describe each book.

Show the lines and corners.

Open it . . . close it.

Fan the pages.

84

Sing your favorite lullaby.

Sing it to baby.

Does he like it?

Repeat 6 times.

Sit across from baby.

Show baby 3 crackers ... the shape, color and number.

Let baby smell each one.

Crunch the crackers so baby can hear.

Let baby smell again.

Show how many pieces you made.

Repeat 2 times.

Holding baby, walk through the rooms of the house.

Open drawers and say "open."

Shut drawers and say "shut."

Watch baby watching the action.

Repeat 2 times.

Show baby a colorful book.

Point out as many items as you both can see that are green.

Say "this is a green hat ..."

Say "this is a green truck ..."

And so on.

Brain Fact:
While the brain is receiving a message, it is measuring truth or value by observing tone and gestures.

Gently hold baby's hands.

Gently bring them together to touch.

Say "clap." Say "patticake." Sing the rhyme.

Repeat 3 times.

Face baby, smile and make eye contact.

Now, stretch your neck and head UP.

Now DOWN, now to the RIGHT, now to the LEFT.

Say "up, down, right, left."

Observe. Do baby's eyes follow you?

Repeat slowly and observe 3 times.

Show baby, when he is sitting across from you, watching.

What can fit in a bowl?

Cereal, water, balls of paper . . . many things.

Show baby what you can fit in, then dump out!

Sit across from baby. Make eye contact.
Say each vowel and the word that begins with each vowel.
(Wait between each word for baby to speak.)

A — Apple

E — Eagle

I — Ice

O — Only

U — Universe

Seat baby safely in the room where she can see.

Make toast! Butter it ... mmm!

Talk about it.

Let baby smell the warm bread.

Use a paper plate or paper. Draw dark stars on it. Say "stars."

Let baby enjoy watching the shapes.

Hold it about 8 inches from baby's face
(hold and wait 10 seconds).

Now, move it to the right (hold and wait 10 seconds).

Now, move it to the left (hold and wait 10 seconds).

Repeat.

Slowly pass a bottle of vanilla extract
(used for cooking) under baby's nose.

Describe the smell.

What is baby's reaction?

Repeat 4 times.

Outside with baby, fill up a cup with water.

Pour water in the dirt or sand.

Watch it disappear!

Show baby.

Repeat 5 times.

You can let baby feel the dirt.

Help baby put his fist to his mouth.

Watch him explore the taste.

Put your finger or hand to his mouth.

Watch how he explores.

Hold baby close and kiss his neck.

Let him "kiss" yours.

With baby on your lap, his back leaning on you, hold a large mirror at arm's length.

Look in the mirror with baby and talk about how great you both look!

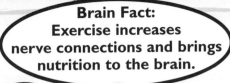

Exercise baby flat on his back, palms gently
outstretched to sides.

Softly bring hands to chest.

Bicycle his legs.

GENTLY repeat each arm and leg 10 times.

Sit across from baby.

Starting with yourself, and then with baby,
touch your hair, then baby's.

Touch your mouth, then baby's, and so on.

Go from head to toe.

Tell baby what you are doing.

Show baby a PEAR.

Say "pear." Take a bite.

Show baby the white fruit and the green skin.

Let baby smell.

Just a teeny taste of juice.

101

Say your baby's name frequently.

When baby responds to his or her name,

respond appropriately.

Smile, hug and praise!

Place some baby oil on your hand.

Let baby smell it. Name the smell.

Let baby's finger touch the oil and describe the slickness and softness to baby.

Rub some oil into baby's arm.

Sit across from baby.

When she is watching, open your mouth ... shut your mouth.

Turn your head to the right.

Turn your head to the left.

Raise your right arm slowly.

Let your arm fall down slowly.

Repeat 3 times.

Hold baby in your arms.

Place your head next to baby's.

Sway and move to a sweet melody.

Whisper or sing to baby, words about your promises, feelings and love.

Massage baby's back.

Use gentle circles, each ending upward
along the side of the spine.

Get a partner. Let baby watch.

Lie on your back and pretend you're the baby.

Partner waves hello, shows a stuffed animal,
shakes a rattle — close and far.

What feels good to "baby?"

What can be changed?

Spend one full minute observing your child.

Tell your child what you see.

(Example: I see you looking at your right hand. You're opening and examining your right fingers. Your face looks "surprised." Your eyes are open very wide.
I see your mouth smile.)

Walk with baby and show him things we use each morning:

Alarm clock, hairbrush, rollers, lipstick, comb, toothbrush, etc.

Besides showing the items, show how they work.

Take a hard-boiled egg and place it in baby's hand.

Keep it in place by cupping your hand under hers.

With your control and help, crack the egg on a hard surface.

Let baby experience the cracking of the shell.

Let baby smell the hard-boiled egg.

Show baby a picture of a person in your memory.

Point out a special feature of this person.

Tell why this person is special to you.

Touch baby's hair and cheek gently.

Touch baby's hand and tell him why he's special to you.

Gather solid and melted items.

Ice and water. Ice cream and liquid. Butter — solid and melted. Popsicle and colored liquid.

Name them. Show baby what can happen. Let baby touch.

Repeat 2 times.

Let baby smell bitter or sour.
(You can pass a jar under baby's nose.)

Try pickles, onions, vinegar, salad dressing. Name the item,
its taste or smell and its color. Say "pickle, sour, green."

Observe baby's reaction. Take time between odors.

Repeat 3 times.

Practice language tone with baby.

Look at baby and ask: How are YOU today?
How ARE you today? How are you TODAY?

Repeat, using a high voice, low voice and a whisper.

Repeat 3 times.

Rub your favorite lotion on your neck, arms and hands.

Let baby smell. Tell baby why you like it.

Hold baby close.

Rock and walk and talk.

Brain Fact:
Skills for math and
logic develop between
ages 0-4 years.

Show baby, when she is sitting safely
across from you and watching:

What can go in a cup?

Fill with cereal — pour out.

Fill with water — pour out.

Fill with cottonballs — pour out.

Talk and repeat exercise.

116

Sit across from baby and make eye contact.

Show wrapping or tissue paper.

Let baby grasp it. Tug gently.

Let paper rip and crinkle.

Stuff paper in a bag and pull it out!

Repeat 3 times.

Play "beach."

Roll a colorful ball across the floor.

Place sand or cornmeal in a flat box.

Draw through it with your fingers.

Let baby step in it.

Take 5 separate pieces of paper. Using only a pencil, make a circle on each one. Decorate simply.

First, show baby.
Let him enjoy looking at different shades and lines.

Second, show each slowly for 8 seconds.
Describe the design again.

Show baby how DIFFERENT actions with hands feel.

Use your hands in his.

Try: touch, pat, swing hands, hold hands.

Name the action.

As you repeat, let baby experience the feel.

Repeat 3 times.

Brain Fact:
When baby can make something happen, she controls her environment — which increases self-esteem!

Attach a bell to a brightly colored sock.

This is perfect for babies who are just bringing their legs up and squirming.

Baby will love to shake her feet!

Make attachment secure, and monitor for safety!

Show baby a carrot. Name the color. Let baby hold the
carrot. Let baby smell the carrot.

Give baby a taste of mashed carrots, or (depending on age)
let lips touch the cleaned whole carrot.

Make eye contact with baby.

Gently stroke baby's arm and each finger.

Tell baby what you're doing:

"I'm touching your arm . . . I'm touching each finger."

Repeat slowly 2 times.

Name the pieces of clothing you have on.

Name the kind of cloth the pieces are made of.

Tell baby what you do when you wear these clothes.

Let baby touch these different materials.

Watch the TV cartoon channel for dance and sing-along ideas.

BUT

Be sure to sit with baby and actually sing along!

Obtain a clear soda bottle that has a top.

Fill it half way with water and cap it.

Show baby how the water flows and the bubbles it makes when you turn it up and down.

What does it sound like?

With baby sitting comfortably or lying down,
encourage him to focus on a ribbon you are holding.

Move it slowly across his line of vision. Name it "ribbon."
Allow it to gently touch baby's hand or arm.

Describe the color and feeling (blue, thin, tickle)

Repeat slowly 6 times.

Sit facing baby so she sees your eyes and mouth.

Sing in your regular voice this melody: la la LA la la.
(Repeat it twice.)

Sing it in a high voice, then in a low voice.

A high voice quickly, a low voice slowly.

After each sing, wait for baby's response.

Sit baby across from you. Make eye contact.

Name a piece of laundry and hold it up.

Fold it and show its changed shape.

(Example: Fold a blanket into a smaller square.)

Fold a T-shirt, tucking in the sleeves.

Repeat 3 times.

Peel a banana. Let baby see and smell. Slice or mash the banana. Let baby smell the sweet odor by passing it under her nose.

Say "banana." Say "yellow and white."

Describe the shape, whole, mashed and sliced.

If baby is old enough, give her a taste.

While holding baby, watch the rain outside.

Describe the rain sound or make your own.

Turn on the shower and compare it to rain.

Let baby feel the sprinkle of water on her hand,
foot and face.

Make eye contact.

Talk to baby about how a good parent teaches a baby to be "independent."

Play with 2 favorite toys.

Tell baby about one special thing you'll do together on your next "free" day.

Vision!

Show baby a colorful picture or a real American flag.

Point out the white and red stripes.

Trace out the star shapes on the blue background.

Describe the colors and contrasts.

Wave the flag!

Vision!

Hold or position baby safely.

Flip the light switch on and off.

Watch how baby observes each.

Say "on, off, light, dark."

Talk about why we use a light switch.

Give baby's eyes time to adjust with each on or off switch.

When the sink is empty and you are holding baby safely at the front edge, let her watch and listen as water pours into the sink and goes down the drain.

Refill and describe 5 times.

While you are holding your baby, show him
the washer and dryer. Tell about washing clothes.

Let baby see the sudsing and listen to the drying.

When the tops are closed, you can let baby sit safely on
the top, feeling the vibration, the warmth and the action.

With baby watching and these items already nearby,
show and describe the differences:

A solid item — ice. A liquid item — water.

Dry oatmeal. Cooked oatmeal.

Let baby smell and touch if cool.

Repeat 2 times.

Slowly slide a silk object across baby's arms and legs.

Describe the feeling (smooth, soft).

Does baby like it? Does he look pleased?

Talk about the feeling.

Repeat 4 times.

Spell baby's name on a piece of paper in bold letters.

Show baby. Point out each letter and say the name out loud.

Watch to see baby looking at where you are pointing.

Repeat 4 times.

Brain Fact:
Babies connect emotions to words before they relate meaning.

Sit across from baby.

Share a picture and your voice that tells a mood.

"My voice is like this when I'm: (make the voice sounds) sad, tired, disappointed, irritated."

Sit baby upright where he can see you.

Show baby one macaroni and say "one macaroni."

Show baby many macaronies in a clear glass.

Show baby one pencil and say "one pencil."

Roll many pencils through your fingers.

Repeat 3 times.

Put several items in a shoe box (pencil, crayons, marker, pen).

Older children look, touch and smell.

Younger children look and smell.

Repeat names and smells 5 times.

Pick 2 items to repeat daily.

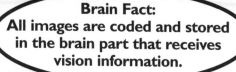

Brain Fact:
All images are coded and stored
in the brain part that receives
vision information.

Gather 4 boxes of various sizes.
(You can put presents in them later.)

Fit the smaller in the larger.

As baby watches and you explain,
take off each top to reveal the smaller box inside.

Let baby put her hand inside.

Repeat all steps 3 times.

Let baby "mouth" or feel on his skin the different
textures of several clean cotton cloths.

Try a washcloth, a dish towel,
a cloth diaper, a T-shirt, a blanket.

Repeat 2 times.

Hold a book and fan the pages.

Tell baby to smell the paper.

Rustle a newspaper and show baby.

Tell baby to smell news print.

Flip through a magazine. Let baby smell the pictures.

Repeat the different smells 2 times.

Show baby an orange. Name everything about it.

Describe the shape, and let baby touch and smell it.

Peel the skin and let baby enjoy the aroma on your hands.

Show baby all the pieces that fit together!

Play "beach."

Gently splash baby's feet in water.

Lay him on a towel.

Play an "ocean" tape or make your own "wave" sounds.

Blow gently on baby's arms like a gentle sea breeze.

Show baby and describe these sounds we make
(you can use water):

Gulping. Gargling. Sipping.
Slurping. Spitting. Spraying. Laughing.

Repeat 2 times.

Lay baby on your lap or on a blanket.

Rub his back gently up and down, and round and round.

Use a simple rhyme to set the pace.

Repeat 3 times.

Sit with baby and look at the cars going by.

Talk about the cars.

Make up a story about where the cars are taking the people.

Sit baby across from you and make eye contact.

Tell baby what you are going to do.

Fan baby with a piece of paper. Gently blow air on baby.

Describe the effect — "breeze, fan, air, cool."

Does baby like it?

If so, repeat each 2 times.

Use different tones for the words, as you sit baby across from you, and say:

You are so smart and special.

YOU are so smart and special.

You are SO smart and special.

You are so SMART and special.

You are so smart and SPECIAL.

Tell baby a short story about your day.

Holding baby, rock gently forward to the count of 10.

Rock to the right (count to 10).

Rock to the left (count to 10).

Repeat.

Make eye contact with baby.

Talk about learning her "cues" — how you notice when she cries, or fusses, or reaches, she is telling you something.

Let baby touch a toy. Can she reach?

Repeat with 3 toys.

Read a page from baby's favorite book.

Re-read the page 4 times.

Brain Fact:
A full one-quarter of the
brain is devoted to vision!

With baby watching and these items already nearby,
show and describe and demonstrate.

Say the words:

A "flexible" item — cheese.

A "firm" item — a metal spoon.

A "light" item — tissue paper.

A "heavy" item — bracelet.

Show baby a door and a window near each other.

Knock on the door. Knock on the window.

Show how they open. Wave your hand through the space.

Close them again. Say the words and describe:
"Door/window, open/closed."

Repeat 2 times.

Put a familiar perfume on a cotton ball.
(You could store it in a sealed plastic bag.)

Place a familiar cologne on cotton in another bag.

Put a cotton ball with baby oil in another bag.

Allow baby to smell each one, naming the familiar person.

Repeat 2 times.

Show baby a shoe box with lid, a sealed plastic bag and a plastic storage container with lid.

Show baby how lids snap off and on, bags zip and unzip.

Repeat 4 times.

Show baby a whole peach. Let her smell it.

Let her put her mouth on clean peach skin.

Show peach slices and let baby smell them.

Put a taste of peach juice on your finger and let baby have a bit, if she is old enough.

If you show the baby food jar, show the color peach and the picture of the smiling baby.

Taste!

Let baby "mouth" (taste) clean items
to experience taste and texture.

Try a plastic cup, a wooden spoon, a glass, a metal spoon.

You can describe each item, using words like cool, warm, slick.

Repeat 3 times.

Draw a picture or show a whole pineapple.

Describe the fruit outside:

Rough, spiky, prickly.

Cut and show pieces of bright yellow fruit.

Let baby smell and touch.

Lay baby down in front of you.

Make eye contact and smile. Cover her hands with yours.

Pat hands together (1-2-3). Apart (1-2-3).

Put her feet in your hands.

Pat together (1-2-3). Apart (1-2-3).

Repeat 3 times.

Tell baby how you "work" at your jobs.

Demonstrate the keys and screen of your computer, or let baby watch while you demonstrate scrubbing the tub with a sponge and cleanser.

Or, show baby under the hood of the car where you fix the parts.

Describe, show and explain.

Pick 3 jobs to share.

Sit with baby and watch the cars going by.

Point to the RED ones.

Say "red, red car."

Point to the BLACK ones and say "black, black car."

Point out dogs, cats and other animals from a book of pictures.

Name the animal. Give the animal sound with each picture.

Wait and watch baby between sounds.

Repeat each animal picture 3 times.

Place 4 small items (SMALLER than his hand) in baby's hand.

Place them one at a time.

Allow baby to experience how each feels. Be safe.

Try a penny, a macaroni, a cereal, a raisin.

Use the words smaller/bigger.

Repeat slowly 2 times.

Guide baby's hand to touch a stuffed animal.

Describe the feel of fur.

How to touch? Say "gently."

Watch baby's expression.

Help baby touch and name (eyes, feet, tail).

With baby on her back, have her look at
a brightly colored rattle or toy.

Tell baby you are going to watch her "track" the toy.

Move the toy in a small arc before your baby's eyes.

Each time make the arc larger so baby will have to turn.

Move slowly.

With a dark marker, draw thin black lines on the right half of one piece of paper. Draw thick black lines on the left half of another piece of paper.

Sit across from baby.

Move the first page slowly from right to left, and then left to right. Observe baby as he watches. Move the second piece of paper slowly from left to right, and from right to left.

Repeat 3 times.

Let baby smell 3 soaps (bar, detergent and dishwashing soaps).

Describe the smells.

You might also add a description of the sensation of touch to each soap (smooth and flat, dry particles, liquid and slick).

Repeat 2 times.

Place baby in a safe sitting position, where she can see you.
Walk across the room. Allow her eyes to follow you.
Sit in a chair, stand up, sit down. Do it a second time.

Describe what you are doing.

Do it a third time.

Use words like UP, DOWN, SIT and STAND.

Show baby a plain paper plate. Color it orange,
and show it again. Draw black triangle eyes and a nose.

Show baby. Point out the triangles with your finger.

Say "triangles."

Cut out the triangles and show baby the new "air" triangles.

Place the paper plate over your face, if baby enjoys.

Read a paragraph or story from a magazine
while baby is sitting with you.

Read the paragraph over 3 times.

Baby will enjoy being close to you and the sound of your voice.

Show baby the pictures, too.

Gather some fall leaves.

Show each one to baby.

Say "green, red, orange, yellow, brown."

Drop them, one by one, from your hand to show baby "fall."

Repeat 4 times.

Cut out a black square and a white square of paper.

Attach to both sides of a popsicle stick.

Show baby the black square and say "black."

Turn the stick to show baby the white square and say "white."

Repeat 5 times.

Touch!

Sit across from baby.

Touch her and her clothes gently.

Describe and touch, saying things like:

"Buttons are here, snaps are here. The green color is on the stripes here. The shorts have elastic here . . ."

Repeat.

Put sand in a baggie. Place stones, shiny pennies and foil balls in with the sand.

Help baby discover the objects in the sand.

Does baby like one better than the other?

(Note: ALWAYS monitor closely when a child is handling small objects.)

Dribble or spoon warm water over baby's legs and feet during a relaxed bath.

Talk about the soothing sensation.

Set baby up in the kitchen where she is safe,
but can see you.

Tell about the wonderful smells of cooking.

Name the item and its color.

With baby sitting across from you, talk about transportation.

Use your fingers, hands and arms to make the movements
of walking, riding a bike, a train, a bus, a plane.

Repeat 3 times.

Help baby exercise the voice and mouth.

Sit baby across from you and make eye contact. Smile.

Make a "clucking" noise. Make "raspberries." Laugh.

Take note: Does baby imitate you?

Repeat 4 times.

Get ready to make a sandwich.

One at a time, let baby smell: jelly, bread and peanut butter.

Tell her what each one is and
pause to let her take in the smell.

Repeat 2 times.

Show baby the mounds of pumpkins for sale at a store or vegetable stand.

Describe the pumpkins: orange, green, ridges, bumpy, smooth.

If you carve one, let baby smell it.

Let him feel and see the cut-outs. Bake a pumpkin pie.

Mmmm, smells good!

Show baby that the physical characteristics of things that are different. (Help him feel them with his finger.)

Firm: a book. Flexible: a magazine.

Light: a piece of tissue. Heavy: your watch.

Let each item rest lightly on baby's hand.

Repeat 3 times.

Hold baby on your lap while you read the news.

Baby will enjoy the sound of your voice.

Baby will enjoy the black and white contrast of the newspaper.

Read an article twice.

The paper makes a nice crinkly sound.

Sit baby comfortably to see you.

Show how to get something in the kitchen.

Cereal: Open the cabinet.

Milk: Open the refrigerator and pour a glassful.

Turn on the water and rinse out the glass.

Explain open, pour, rinse.

Repeat.

187

Brain Fact:
Baby learns by "doing."
Give him lots to do!

Hold baby. Go out and sit in a car.

Demonstrate and name the actions.

Baby will hear: the horn, the wheel, the window,
the turn signal, the inside light, the windshield wiper.

Take a walk with baby.

Describe the trees and changing leaves.

Kick through loose leaves.

Crumple dry leaves through your hands.

Describe the crunch and crinkle.

Let baby smell the Fall leaves.

Fill a clear bottle (with cap) with water. Add color.

Try ketchup, mustard, or food coloring. Shake the water and coloring. Show baby the colored water.

Turn it up, turn it down.

Repeat.

Press baby's fingers into a soapy sponge.

Observe the reaction to the sound and feel.

Describe the sound (squish!).

Describe the feel (slick, slippery).

Repeat several times.

Lightly, gently, brush baby's fingers over a piece of coarse sandpaper, or maybe an emery board.

Describe the feel. Rough? Scratchy?

Watch baby's reaction.

Repeat gently.

Sit baby across from you.

Make good eye contact.

Make the motor noises for getting around.

Show or draw a picture.

Try walking, riding a bike, a train, a bus, a plane.

Remember to check baby's face for expression.

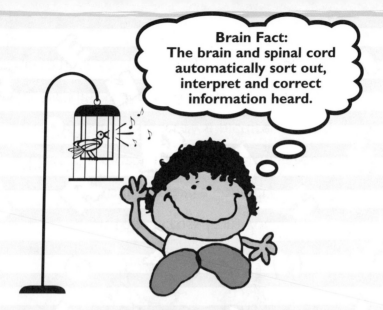

Help baby hold a measuring spoon set or a rattle.

Can baby jingle the spoons or make a noise with the rattle?

Help her if she can't. Name the noise.

Say "Listen . . . did you hear that?
You made that noise! You did very well!"

Holding baby comfortably so he can see forward:

Open the refrigerator. Close it.

Say "open." Say "shut."

Now open.

Describe and point to colorful food.

Is the air cool?

Place a favorite doll or stuffed animal on a chair
in the middle of the room.

Walk and sit with baby to see and describe how it looks:

From above, from in front, from behind,
and from below it on the floor.

Give baby time to see how things look different and the same.

Set out an ice cream container, margarine container
and jelly jar. Help baby stick a finger in each,
or rub a small bit in baby's hand.
Describe textures (soft, squishy . . .).

Say "This is jelly. It's soft, sticky, red, sweet."

"This is margarine . . . this is ice cream."

Repeat 3 times.

Show baby some pieces of a green bean.

Let baby smell by passing the bean under baby's nose.

Name the vegetable.

Name its color and what it tastes like.

Let baby's lips touch the bean.

Let her taste if she is old enough.

Sit on the floor with baby.

Put out 3 different toys.

Take turns covering them with a blanket.

Show baby when they are in sight.

Point out when they are gone (covered).

Repeat 3 times.

Draw a plain snowman on a piece of paper. Show baby. Name it "snowman."

Then draw on the decorations:

Buttons, pipe, hat, scarf, carrot nose.

Let baby enjoy the shapes.

Name the decorations.

Sing "Frosty the Snowman."

Before dinner, sit baby in a safe place
to watch as you go about fixing a meal
(or if you are on the clean-up crew).

Talk to baby. Make eye contact and describe
what you are doing and what you are using.

Sit quietly with baby. Close your eyes. What do you hear?

The washing machine spinning? Water running?

Birds singing out the window? A dog breathing?
A car passing by?

Listen and identify 5 sounds. Baby can hear them, too.

Repeat.

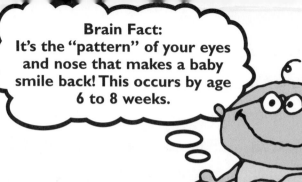

Brain Fact:
It's the "pattern" of your eyes and nose that makes a baby smile back! This occurs by age 6 to 8 weeks.

Sit across from your baby.

Sit quietly and smile.

Observe what baby does. Take your time.

Does baby's finger move up? Move yours.

Does baby blink? Blink back.

Does baby coo? Coo back!

Tell baby you are making bubbles.

Show her how you lather your hands with dishwashing soap.

Show baby how the bubbles can travel by waving your hand.

Repeat. Let baby touch a bubble.

Repeat. Blow the bubbles from your hand.

While baby is watching, repeat the word "bubble."

Mark two pieces of paper with the first letter of baby's name.

Make one letter big, one little (for example, B and b).

Show them to baby at the same level.

Which one is she more attracted to?

Put them down.

Repeat 3 times.

Draw or show a clump of grapes. Show how many grow in a bunch. Pick off one and show baby its shape. Let baby smell the bunch of grapes.

Are they green? Purple? Red?

Let baby feel how smooth and round the grape is in his hand.

Repeat 2 times.

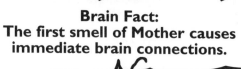

Brain Fact:
The first smell of Mother causes
immediate brain connections.

Take quiet time to breathe in the special smell
of baby's head, neck and arms.

Describe this nice baby smell out loud?

Hold baby comfortably close.

Baby knows your special scent.

Encourage back-and-forth conversation:

Sit across from baby. Make eye contact.

Make a "kiss" sound. Repeat. Wait for baby.

Make a "smack" sound with your lips.

Make a click sound with your tongue. Wait for baby.

Make a cluck sound with your tongue.

Wait for baby to talk!

More About
BRAIN POWER

MORE About the FIVE SENSES
(Hearing, Sight, Smell, Taste and Touch)

A large part of the infant's brain needs information from the "senses" in order to link together correctly.

The FIVE SENSES outline the boundaries of our human world.

Senses (using ears, eyes, nose, mouth and hands) are like "stations".

The "stations" send a signal to the brain which makes SENSE of the information.

MORE About the FIVE SENSES
(Hearing, Sight, Smell, Taste and Touch)

• The brain is divided into parts, like a map.

• The maps divide information.

• The brain has at least 5 "vision maps."

• They divide whole pictures, parts, colors, form and motions.

• Two "hearing maps" in the brain divide similar sounds from other sounds.

• The mouth has many nerve endings! Besides taste, baby learns texture, shape and size.

• When a child "hears," his body can move in rhythm.

• "Smell" molecules tell the brain a memory.

Windows of Opportunity

Recent information tells us there is a "window of opportunity" when brain cell connections MUST be made for some functions to ever occur!

Window of Opportunity for:	Child's Age
Logic	Birth to 4 years.
Speech	Birth to 10 years. Critical period for the spoken word is lost after age 10.
Language	Birth to 12 months. Connections for sound are wired.
Vision	2 to 4 month spurt. Peaks at 8 months.
Music	3 to 10 years

MORE About the Language Window

Hearing is the gateway to language; ears hear but the brain listens.

While awake your child is ALWAYS listening.
The infant brain automatically:

- Sorts information
- Checks levels of awareness and focus
- Checks near and far sound differences
- Scans sequence (what came first or last)
- Classifies and integrates
- Organizes and identifies
- Memorizes for recall

Newborns are "tuned in" to human sound. At six months, they are tuned to their own language. The "critical" period for learning spoken words is **TOTALLY LOST** if not activated by 10 years of age.

MORE About Hearing and the Language Window

A foreign language is most easily learned before age 10.

When telling your child about sounds make them natural.

Repeat sounds throughout the day.

Describe what's happening as often as possible.

Children need to "hear" normal speech to learn it. Most children can take a while to process what is being spoken to them so give them time to listen and learn.

MORE About Music and the Logical Brain

- Few concert violinists started after 10 years of age.

- Early music training alters the brain's anatomy.

- Adults can learn, but it's HARDER because the "WINDOW OF OPPORTUNITY" in early childhood has been missed.

- Music, like language, is organized "sound."

- Pleasant music is produced by strings that have mathematical relationships to each other. The sound waves make up the notes!

- The part of the brain stimulated by music is next to the part of the brain dedicated to math.

- Play Mozart (or any classical music). It might make your baby smarter in math!

MORE About The Vision Window

- Vision is critical during the first year of life.

- Brain connections for vision quickly form between 2 to 4 months, and circuit networks peak at 8 months.

- The vision "window" and hearing development do better together.

- Provide your child with a variety of experiences where you "show and describe" at the same time.

- Brain cells that process vision learn only if baby is given lots to see!

- Make eye contact and be sure your baby is seeing.

Health Notes for Better Growth!

_____

_____

_____

_____

_____

_____

_____

_____

_____

_____

If you are pregnant
and smoke, drink or use drugs . . .

PLEASE STOP TODAY!

VISION

- Infant eyes must be checked at birth and regularly thereafter to be sure vision is occurring.

- Doctors must remove cataracts promptly because they block vision development.

- Have eye infections treated at once!

HEARING

- Let your doctor know if you think baby is not hearing.

- Hearing problems can impair the ability to match sounds to letters.

- Treat ear infections right away!

EXERCISE

- Children who exercise regularly do better in school.

STRESS

- Keep your own stress level down ... then baby will feel free to ask for what he really needs.

- Check with your doctor if baby is losing weight. This can be a sign baby senses a caregiver is too stressed to care for him.

- Touch and massage can release hormones that can ease pain and clear the mind.

- A happy and relaxed environment makes for the best brain connections.

- Infants learn best when they feel safe by having their needs met PROMPTLY and with care.

EXPOSURE TO VIOLENCE CAN STOP CONNECTIONS.

NEVER, NEVER SHAKE A BABY!!

Baby's brain is very delicate.

Shaking can cause bruises and rips in a baby's brain.

DEPRESSION

- Babies who are regularly "under-stimulated" can become depressed.

- Mild retardation is generally believed to be caused by caregiver's failure to provide brain experiences.

- Deprive a baby of touch ... and his body will stop growing.

- To develop fully, infants need "responding" adults in their lives.

- Food for the brain:

STIMULATION
EYE CONTACT
HOLDING
SOUNDS
GENTLE TOUCH

PREMATURE INFANTS

- May not respond or perceive sounds easily.

- May have difficulty sorting or screening sounds.

- May become overloaded and overstimulated.

WHAT HAPPENS?

- Baby cannot focus on or respond appropriately to incoming information.

- Baby gets fussy, irritable or disorganized.

- Caregivers get frustrated.

WHAT TO DO?

- **RELAX** ... let baby calm down.

- **REDUCE** all incoming physical, auditory and visual messages.

- Spend **QUIET,** gentle time.

- **TRY ACTIVITY AGAIN** when baby is older.

DON'T STOP LEARNING AND HAVING NEW EXPERIENCES!

The brain <u>can</u> take in
new knowledge throughout life.

GOOD TOYS TO TRY

0-3 months
Mobiles, wind chimes and soft animals

3-6 months
Rattles, things to exercise feet and hands

6-9 months
Nesting cups, boxes and bowls, teethers, textured balls and toys that make noise

9-12 months
Books, toys that pull or push and toys that show an action and its result

REFERENCES

Arnold Palmer Hospital for Children and Women. <u>Healthy Start Perspectives</u>. Spring 1997, (4) 1.

Beck, J. "Baby's Brain: Use It or Lose It." <u>The Tampa Tribune</u> October, 1997.

Begley, S. "How To Build a Baby's Brain." <u>Newsweek</u> Spring/Summer, 1997: 28-32.

Begley, S. "Your Child's Brain." <u>Newsweek</u> February, 1996: 55-62.

Bowden, R. <u>The Magical Years: The Bowden Method at Home</u>. Nashville, TN: The Southwestern Co., 1989.

Brisbane, E. H. <u>The Developing Child</u>. Mission Hill: Glencoe/McGraw-Hill, 1989.

Brownlee, S. and Watson, T. "The Senses." <u>U.S. News & World Report</u> 1997: 51-59.

Carnegie Corporation. <u>Starting Points: Meeting the Needs of Our Youngest Children</u>. New York, NY: Carnegie Task Force on meeting the needs of young children, 1994.

Executive Producer Craig, S., and Producer Giangreco, K. <u>Ten Things Every Child Needs</u> [Film] Chicago: WTTW Channel 11, 1977.

Education Commission of the States and The Charles A. Dana Foundation. <u>Bridging the Gap Between Neuroscience and Education</u>. Denver, CO: 1996.

Education Commission of the States and The Charles A. Dana Foundation. <u>Neuroscience Research Has Impact for Education Policy</u>. Denver, CO: 1996.

Education Commission of the States. <u>State Education Leader</u>. Denver, CO: 1997.

Ellison, S. and Fernandi, S. <u>365 Days of Baby Love</u>. Naperville, IL: Sourcebooks, Inc., 1996.

Families & Work Institute. <u>Rethinking the Brain: New Insights Into Early Development</u>. "Brain Development in Young Children: New Frontiers for Research, Policy and Practice." University of Chicago, 1996.

REFERENCES

Florida. Florida Department of Education. <u>The Caregiving Environment – Planning an Effective Program. Florida Department of Education</u>: Model of Interdisciplinary Training for Children with Handicaps. Tallahassee: Florida Department of Education, 1990.

Jabs, C. "Your Baby's Brainpower." <u>Working Mother</u> Nov. 1996: 25-28.

Jensen, E. <u>Brain Compatible Strategies</u>. Del Mar, CA: Turning Point Publishing, 1997.

Klas, E. M. "And Baby Makes Three." <u>Florida Trend</u> Oct. 1997: 100-107.

Kotulak, R. <u>Inside the Brain</u>. Kansas City, MO: Andrews McMeel Universal Co., 1996.

Martin, E. <u>Baby Games</u>. Philadelphia, PA: Running Press, 1988.

"Massage Helps Newborns Feeling Mom's Depression." <u>The Orlando Sentinel</u> July 1997.

Nash, M. J. "Fertile Minds." <u>Time</u> 3 Feb. 1997: 48-56.

"Research Shows Babies, Kids Develop Brain Power." <u>The Tampa Tribune</u> Oct. 1996, A1, A14.

Staso PH.D., W. H. <u>What Stimulation Your Baby Needs to Become Smart</u>. Santa Maria: Great Beginnings Press, 1995.

Stern, Daniel. <u>Interpersonal World of the Infant: A View from Psychoanalysis and Developmental Psychology</u>. New York: Basic Books, 2000.

The Growth and Development Corporation. <u>Baby Works</u>. Middletown: Field Publication, 1989.

"The Reasons Why We Need to Rely Less on Day Care." <u>The Washington Post</u> October 1998, C1.

University of Washington, School of Nursing. <u>NCAST Caregiver/Parent-Child Interaction Teaching Manual</u>. Seattle: NCAST Publications, 1994.

ZERO TO THREE. <u>New Visions for the Developmental Assessment of Infants and Young Children</u>. Washington DC: Zero to Three Press, 1996.

NEED ADDITIONAL COPIES?

1-877-992-7246
1-877-99 BRAIN

Major credit cards accepted.

Quantity discounts are available!

About BETA …

Everyone involved in the creation of this book are staff members and volunteers of BETA Center, Inc., in Orlando, Florida.

BETA Center is a private, non-denominational, social service agency that has served the Central Florida area since 1976. BETA provides therapeutic and educational services for adolescents, their children and women who are pregnant and parenting. This 29-year commitment to provide innovative quality programs has resulted in the development of this book. Our agency goal is to empower people. This book is one way to empower parents to improve parent-child attachment, provide information on brain development and play with baby.

It is our hope that all parents will enjoy and enhance their experiences with their children by the use of this book.

Kathy Icardi Hummel, MSW, L.C.S.W.
Executive Vice President, BETA Center